The Poetry of John Lucas Tupper

John Lucas Tupper was born at some point between 1823 and 1824, there are no more precise details recorded.

The family business was that of printers and stationers. His father, George Frederic Tupper, who was trained as a lithographic draftsman, owned his own firm, and his two older sons, George and Alexander, worked there. Tupper's brother undertook the first printing of The Germ (The Pre-Raphaelite magazine) and, subsequently, its publication (largely, one suspects, to provide their brother with a means of publishing his writings.)

Tupper was a student at the Royal Academy and supported himself with his work at Guy's Hospital between 1849 and 1863, initially as an anatomical draftsman. He attempted a career as a sculptor and showed eleven portrait medallions at the annual Royal Academy Exhibitions between 1854 and 1868, and received a commission for his most important sculpture, the "Linnaeus," in 1856.

In 1863 Tupper left Guy's Hospital to become a drawing teacher at the University of London. From 1865 until his death, he served as drawing master for geometrical or scientific drawing at Rugby, which ensured the financial security for him to pursue his artistic endeavours. While at Rugby he wrote The True Story of Mrs Stowe (about Byron), and Hiatus, or the Void in Modern Education under the name "Outis," meaning "no man." In 1871 he published an article on Woolner in the Portfolio.

He married Annie Amelia French and they had two children, one of whom, Holman, he named after his friend William Holman Hunt, who was his son's godfather.

Whilst Tupper was not a major figure in the Pre-Raphaelites, he was certainly influential and his poetry was admired by many.

Tupper was the only member of the Pre-Raphaelite circle with interests in both art and science and in the course of his career he published poetry, art criticism, book reviews, and a treatise on art education.

After a period of ill health John Lucas Tupper died on 29th September 1879.

Index of Contents

Books and writings about the "Pre-Rraphaelite Brotherhood," which was established in the autumn of 1848, are by this time tolerably numerous. Among them, here and there, occurs the name of John Lucas Tupper, and some faint suggestion of who he was and what he did. The time seems to have come at last for impressing his name more definitely upon the public memory, and for indicating — and indeed, I think, proving — that he was a man with a very considerable poetic gift of his own, and highly deserving of explicit and honourable record.

I will only cite one testimony to John Tupper's claims as a poet. In the book which I published in 1895 — "Dante Gabriel Rossetti, his Family Letters, with a Memoir" — occurs a note to the following effect: "There was a little lyric of Tupper's on the Garden of Eden in ruinous decay, of which Dante Rossetti thought very highly. He compared it to Ebenezer Jones's lyric, 'When the world is burning'; and said that, had it been the writing of Edgar Poe, it would have enjoyed world-wide celebrity."

John Lucas Tupper was born in London in or about 1826. It may perhaps be as well to say at the outset that he had no sort of de facto connection with Martin Farquhar Tupper, the author of "Proverbial Philosophy, " although it is said that the two men were "eleventh cousins." His father was a lithographic and general printer in the city of London, and the business is still kept up by two of John's brothers. John Tupper, exhibiting an early bias towards the arts of design, became a student at the Royal Academy. He was, I think, rather undecided for a while whether he should take to painting or to sculpture; ultimately he settled upon the latter. In the Academy classes he became known to the young artists who formed the Pre-Raphaelite Brotherhood — Millais, Holman Hunt, Woolner, Stephens, Collinson, and Dante Rossetti: Hunt and Stephens, and after a time Rossetti, more particularly knew him well. My own introduction to him may have taken place early in 1849; by that date, without abandoning the sculptural profession, he had shunted himself off into a special line of work, being installed as anatomical draughtsman at Guy's Hospital — an employment for which he was exceptionally well qualified. As a young man he exhibited a few sculptural works at the Royal Academy, and perhaps elsewhere — works showing advanced studentship and the severest tenets of truthful rendering — but nothing of his ever fixed the public attention. The tendency of his mind was certainly quite as much scientific as artistic; and, though I conceive him to have been fully capable of producing sound works of art, had circumstances been favourable, he did in fact pass through life without realizing anything considerable in sculpture, if we except the life-sized statue of Linnaeus in the Oxford University Museum — a work of the most conscientious order in realism of intention and unsparing precision of detail.

Quitting Guy's Hospital in 1863, Mr. Tupper received, in March 1865, the appointment of Master of the classes for geometrical or scientific drawing at Rugby School; where he was distinguished for solid and ingenious learning, zealous devotion to his work, and successful training of his pupils. He married in 1871 (the last day of the year), and has left a widow and two children. At Rugby he died on September 29th 1879. His health had for some years been precarious, more especially after a very dangerous illness of a spasmodic or convulsive kind which attacked him in Florence in 1869, when I was his travelling-companion.

A man of stricter principle than John Tupper, more bent upon doing right, more honourable in act, more tenacious of the truth as he discerned it, has not been known to me. He was not without ambition, founded upon a well-justified, but always very modest, consciousness of abilities — scientific, artistic, speculative, poetical; and yet was content with his rather secluded and inconspicuous lot in life. He was a steadfast and affectionate friend, as no one knows better than myself.

Even before I knew him in 1849, Tupper had written a good deal of verse. The Pre-Raphaelite magazine, "The Germ," issued in 1850, and printed by the Tupper firm, contains the following contributions of his: in verse, " A Sketch from Nature, " " Viola and Olivia," and two humorous sketches, "An Incident in the Siege of Troy," and "Smoke"; in prose, "The Subject in Art."

Perhaps one of the most marked symptoms of poetical temperament is an acute susceptibility to impressions. A scene or an object in nature, a human personality or passion, is discerned, and discerned with peculiar vividness; but the matter does not remain there — the perception of the eye and mind becomes an impression on the whole individuality of the poet, the nutriment of his emotion, and of his fancy or imagination, which swathe it like a lambent flame. That which entered into him as a perception issues forth as a transmuted entity — real, and also visionary. I apprehend that this poetical quality is strongly, and even rather abnormally, marked in the verse of John Tupper. There is also, in various instances, a true lyrical impetus, and a certain cosmic feeling, to which his peculiar turn for science (contemplated rather in the abstract than merely physically) contributed. A repugnance to some aspects of modernism, whether in the domain of physics or of mind, will be observed here and there. A few of the poems now collected are humorous (these are grouped together in the latter half of the volume): they have, I think, a genuine mingling of oddity and sprightliness, or what we call quaintness. The general tone and tenor of Tupper's poetry is summed up not inaptly in his sonnet "To Annie" (his wife), where he speaks of himself as singing of

"Rarest things
That make the earth a perfume and a song,
And of vague solace of imaginings."

John Tupper did not during his lifetime publish any volume of verse; and it appears to me that, after the date of "The Germ," scarcely anything of his, in the poetic form, got into print, even in magazines etc. He left, however, a substantial bulk of verse, which his widow copied out — no light task. Her copies form the manuscripts which have come into my hands. Some of the pieces, besides being confusedly jotted down by himself, had obviously not received his final revision; and I have thought it not only a right but a duty to rectify here and there some stumble of metre or of diction, or some lapse of rhyme. The reader may rely upon it that what I have thus done is really a trifle, and not such as to impair in any appreciable degree the authenticity of the work. In fact while I should have regarded it as unkind to the memory of my old friend to omit doing what I have done, I should have deemed it impertinence to go beyond this narrow limit.

Mr. Tupper was the author of two published books: in each instance he wrote under the fancy name of "Outis." These are "The True Story of Mrs. Stowe" (concerning Lord Byron), and (1869) "Hiatus, or the Void in Modern Education": the latter received at the time some fair amount of press notice. There are several MS. poems besides those which I have as yet examined; also a prose story and various papers on scientific and other subjects. Possibly some of these may yet see the light of publication.

In the present volume I have added a few notes, but only where there were some allusions etc. which seemed not likely to explain themselves.

W. M. ROSSETTI

LONDON
November 1896.

IN CHILDHOOD

'Twas a god-haunted meadow, grassed and wide;
Poplars grew on the eastern side,
The brown wood rose behind.
It was not low, it was not high.
For the woods all round went higher: the sky
Was next to these; and the sunset blind
Tore through the deepest forestry.

There was no empty plain for the eye
To wander over, remote or nigh.
There was no ground but the meadow grass;
Dusk woods walled out the world somewhere —
Away where no one strove to pass;
And whether there was another sky
Or other earth we did not care.

The sky and the meadow belonged to each other,
The life that I led to me was new
In a world that was new, and the wonder grew.
As the flowers each day
Changed their array,
Or changed into berry and fruit the flower.
Through the long day and hour by hour
I could talk and play and talk with my mother.

And oh it was glad when the evening came
To sit by the small lamp's flickering flame,
And read of a world that was more than a name,
And less than a substance. The histories passed
Of Noah and Enoch and Solomon,
Of Theseus, Alcides and Telamon,
And haunters of forest and fountain and sod.
I grew up in love without method amassed.
Loving, hating, desiring, and wondering,
A haunter of autumn and haunter of spring.
And sometimes conceiving I might be a god.

WIND-NOTES

I will not come to thee,
Although my eyes are tranced
And full of thy dear face.

And on this side the day of doom
We shall not meet, because the world
Works change on what it wears away.

For I design to think of thee
Only as now I think, and so
To think of thee until I die.

For thou to me a sunrise art.
To which a thousand drops of dew
Belong and thousand flowers, —

Which when the thousand drops of dew
And when the thousand flowers are not,
Is not the same sunrise.

Thou art to me a sound of bells
At night — a moment of the night
When winds lift sound away.

Thou art to me the crystal song
Of thrushes to the stars ere morn,
While yet the lawns are white:

Or nightingale's song poured away
Profuse with thunder standing near,
To keep the long night wild:

Or else a sempiternal sky
With nine blue stars in rocking leaves,
And a little golden moon.

SUNRISE

Listen! a sweet bird singing now,
Although it is not light;
He sits on yon acacia bough
To watch the wane of night.
O mystery of mysteries!
What are these festivals and cries
Of birds, of flowers in summer weather?

Badly the dull ear keeps together
Notes flung down from the ple6lral rod,
That thrills all nature with the beat
Of mystic life announcing God,
And wakes the ever a6live heat
Through earth, and tunes the ether-string
That throbs in colour, to make sing
The undulous sea of charmed air.
What shall be deemed of life? O where
Begin its vague interpreting?

Ere night steps down the western stair.
The stir comes over all — along
Our forest tops no lack of song:
All flowers resume their colours fair
When the Light-god comes, and on the string
Whereon he does his messaging
Vibrate their answer keen and clear.
And I, a mere spectator here
Without a function, fear to call
In worship to the Spirit of all.
My tongue would scream a note of woe
At dissonance from nature so;
My voice would be a leaden pall
Upon the glad flowers' golden glow.

A million king-cups mean to flare
Bright eyes to heaven, which turns to flash
A sun back. There will be a clash
Of jubilant branches in the air,
And out of earth will rise a breath
Of gladness, and the only death
Lurks in my heart — no other-where?
Resolve the mystery; bring me aid.
Strange Spirit! Dwelleth harmony
With one? And now thy thought hath made
The shadow of death be dead in me.
Strangely I rise to a ministry —
The mountain pine hath nothing said.

DYING

Beneath the eye of evening, plain
The sleepy hills are lying:
Fields are green from recent rain,
Green the rugged grassy lane.

And how have I wrought on, who die.
Now die, wrung brain in vain
Striving to find them living! Dying,
Look, they come again —
The common, and the children playing
With hoop and bat and bow, the straying
Lambs beyond. So pass them by:
We left them; and we leave them; try
For flowers this rugged grassy lane.
Look, your flowers again!
Why, the flowers you wore for hours —
Not one withered — as I gave them
You, who lost them. I, who have them,
I, who brook no coy gainsaying.
Now have all: the children playing —
All, the sun, the grass, the flowers;
Time — its minutes, hours remain:
I feel the minutes throb again;
Moans the bee, and thrills the bird;
Glimmer sunlit grass and flower;
Flies the white cloud fringed with rain.
So you droop your eyelids lower,
And we have no whisper heard:
So we feel no pain.
And we shut the prison house;
Outside — world, and inside — brain.
Weary world, dark, onerous!
All is here —
A sunset clear:
Eyes clear of scorn, grass fresh with rain.
We'll not wake again!

A WARM FEBRUARY

Over the evening-misty hills
White villas in the stare of the sun:
The heads of elms and chestnuts dun
Take tawny fire, each one by one;
February is not done,
Although the grass is soft and green.
And warm air blows and flows between
These blind bare arms that trees uprear
To feel for summer somewhere near.

Sitting upon the stile, I fain
Would fancy summer up the lane,

Where both the hedges rusty grey
With blackthorn bushes say me nay.
The winter time has left its stain
Of snow upon the thorn and rain
Upon the pales. Like black hairs turning
Grey, it has a look of yearning
Back to youth again.

Oak trees nigh, not 'gainst the sky,
But how black and bare and knotted,
And the sunset clings on high
To the summer mockery
Mournfully bedropped and dotted
Where the ivy dangles by.
And I cannot draw my eyes
From the bare sun-gilded trees,
Because it seems as by degrees
An old grey man is standing there
Letting some damsel trick his hair
As gaily as the sun decks these,
While he bears all without surprise.

And when into the west at last
I turn, the day is sinking fast;
The sun has gapped the hedge with light.
Laid fervid fire on thousand sprays.
Shooting shadows thousand ways
Until they vanish. But the white
Slow mists have muffled up the night,
And all is changed; for now the air
Is chilly, and the moon has shone
Down dimly on a sea unknown.
With sunk rocks visible here and there.
Whereon one cloud-ship sails alone.

A DEATH IN THE FAMILY

Fold up her fan: it will not stir
The air for her.
Outside acacias wave and whirr,
Fanning breaths that pass
From earth to heaven — and what, alas!
Do we with fans?
Also these rings, now? Talismans
Perchance — keep them. We must dispense
With much now useless: whence

A use for what she will not use?
Little things that did amuse.
Employ her daily, no —
Perhaps they should not go;
But all her wardrobe, straight
Hide it. Or, wait —
The sofa with her work thereon
Must not begone:
These tables — she was wont to arrange
Their ornaments. The Grange
Will vanish altogether so.
Trees hold her accents; grass blades know
Her footstep; garden knots, and flowers
Within doors, watered with her hands.
Alas, she leaves us nothing ours
Unsignatured! Dim seas and lands
Remote we needs must seek to be
Remindless of her. For I see
As yet no fleeting cloud along
The rounding verge, hear no faint song
Of wind or bird that doth not say,
"In such attire, on such a day
She pointed, listened."

The dumb ground,
Blind sky, are witnesses around.
The chiming hours will speak in round
That still she hither goes and there;
Her chamber window would not dare
Be bright with daylight if she were
Not in her chamber; every stair
In the still house expect her foot:
And I am conscious, when the mute
Midnight affirms she sleeps, the morn
Will ask for her. To live, and scorn
These witnesses in dumb array?
No— all must go or all must stay.

A SILENT LYRE

No more — no more! It will not sound
The strings relapse with shattering jar,
And leave their mournful whisper. Far
That harp hath travelled over ground
Rugged and smooth — a long way round.

The plectrum now, till music rings!
I feel its weight how dead and cold!
And wonder who could be so bold
As touch with it these delicate strings.
To force out such faint sorrowings.

Sorrowings, submissive, like a wife
To rugged brute intoxicate —
Or flowers, to winds infuriate.
That shed their perfume with their life
Upon the senseless northern knife.

O harp! if I were born anew.
And thou unruined mine again.
The mosses of the calmest rain.
The offspring of the sweetest dew.
Should be too hard, too hard for you.

But something culled from thistle down,
From cygnet plume, or sleepy owl.
With moultage of the eider-fowl.
Wherewith a queen fay lines her crown,
Would shield thee from the loud renown;

Cradle thee soft in solitude.
With nothing save thy will to creep
Self-stirred, in cadence faint or deep,
Through thine own strings in thine own mood.
Unquestioned of the multitude.

Low down within some mountain dell
Where comes not sun, nor wind, and where
Grows dream-like up that maiden-hair
That knows the ghostly twilights well.
There shouldst thou throb inaudible.

EDEN AFTER SIXTY CENTURIES

There are rows of poplars
Down the garden walks;
There are cedars standing
On the dewy lawns;
They have waited many
Mornings of the Spring;
Many swallows fly there,
Many birds sing;

And now is the Summer.

Here be great white lilies
Leaning down their stalks.
The roses like lamps
Standing on their stems,
Burning out their spirit
From morning unto even.
re dying and born.
And all the perfume given
Is given to waste.

The flowers upon the trees
Are mixed with withered flowers,
And black shrivelled seeds
Of last year's growing.
There is no knowing
How long time ago—
If there were hours
And flowers did grow —
A hand took the flowers.

Cystus, anemone,
Olive and myrtle,
Cypress and cinnamon,
Orange and lime.
Go high or low;
And the wandering vine
And ivies entwine.
And stretch at the bough,
The bough of the pine.

The palm tree is weeping.
The gums ever dropping.
The long lawns sleeping.
Nothing is dying.
Growth is not stopping.
Cumbered with nothing.
The low lawns are lying
In their green clothing.

He must be coming.
These must be waiting.
Are the bees not humming?
Are they not translating
The golden pollen
From flower to flower?
Are they not debating

In converse sullen
About the hour?

WHAT THE SUN SEES

Still the great sun gets up and holds a light
That men may see what ugly things they do;
And still the pendent plummet hangeth true;
And still the sky is sempiternal blue:
And man gets older, and there cometh night.

The wind was talking in the poplar trees
Over my head, and in this fashion still.
Nor heard I, for the running of the rill,
The chirp of grasshoppers that count and shrill
Some anguished minutes; but I knew of these

And all the other pain-enforced voice
Of swallow, or expostulating bee;
Because there was no creature I could see.
Or animal, or wind, or shaken tree,
That deemed the sun had reason to rejoice.

Trust me, the river gurgled chokingly.
The mill went jarring round, and blear and dun
Clouds in the eye of the insulting sun
Escaped towards the west: and one by one
Hot sheep rose up, then sank along the lea;

As if they had not rightly settled which.
Motion or rest, were painfuller; and still
The light was everywhere, with prying skill
Demonstrating a present, visible ill.
Though it might lurk in furrow or in ditch: —

Showing the lizard murdered by the rat.
The spider, with his prey, tongued by a toad.
The caterpillar writhing at the goad
Of tugging emmets, black into the road.
The chafer by the cow's hoof trodden flat.

Death everywhere, or pain! — until one deemed
The blessedest of all things must be sleep:
A rest that would continue calm and deep
(Although this shepherd will betray his sheep
Unto the slaughterer). And then it seemed,

As I was walking round that labouring mill.
There came a young girl with a lamb to play.
And she had many flowers which bloom a day
But dare not, though we love them, longer stay.
Because the hours are ravenous to kill.

And eat up all: — which, entering not the head
Of this poor child, had almost changed my mind.
To find a happiness I could not find
Attend such blindness. — But the mill was blind.
Whirled round its sail, and struck her lamb stone dead.

So then I said, "Go home, die in your bed;
Sleep first, the only peace before you die!"
The sail went round, and all the wind did sigh:
The poplars whispering contumeliously
"Of winds below, and calm heaven overhead!"

A VISION OF LINNAEUS

I saw a youth walking upon the hills
In the breme Lapland morning, while the sun
Now swerving upward (as a swallow turns
That has not rested on the earth) emblazed
The close fur wrapping him with gold that rippled
I' the flying wind: what time I certified
His cap of fox-skin, and his coat of deer:
And, as he walked, how he would stay his step.
Against the unconquered wind to scrutinize
The ground with flowers and rare growths mottled o'er
In that high region; and the rocks and pools
Sucked there by spongy herbage — not as a girl
Culling wild flowers, who looks for these alone.
But taking with a wide glance all that was
As each a limb of one great animal.
For whether it were moss or flower or fern.
Or fungus growth of rottenness, the bare
Bleached jaw-bone of some stag, or wind-bleached rock.
Or raven's wing in rocky cleft, or foot
Of hare the eagle-owl left, nesting close:
Each sang keen notes of one great anthem still.
Of which the dominant (man, in health, disease.
Or death) rang joyous, with a cry that rent
The harmony up through sunny air to heaven.
Grandly he walked, or grander stood, the wind

Passing, and great thoughts passing on more swift
Within him, what the world had been and was;
While in his hand the flower, held listlessly,
I saw he saw not, for his soul was rapt —
As one who has fasted feels a lightness go
Throughout his frame, conversing more with air
Than solid earth, and running seems to fly.
I saw him hovering about that hill
Like an alighted eagle, staring round
A strange world with a glory in his gaze:
A visitant who momently we fear
Even while we gaze may find his task complete.
And merge into the skies in mystery.

TO —

"The fairies feed on scent."
(Supper Conversation.)

You say that fairies feed on scent:
And then you stay, and check your speech
For fear lest you should seem to reach
Too near the faery land; —
Too near the spirit-realm for each
To fathom what the fancy meant:
You knew we should not understand.

And so it was, with eyes down bent,
You said "'Twas thus with fairies, when
They lived at least," nor answer then
Followed the argument.

But I have had a fancy since.
Dreaming or musing a vague hour.
That raised up many a faery flower
Cradling its faery queen and prince
At banquet there: and I can say
The fairies feed thus to this day.
Nor need you much misgive the event
When next you teach us faery lore.
For fairies are not less, but more
(So thrive they on this subtile scent);

If you expound their nourishment
To our dull ears, that doubt at first,
All too terrestrially nursed

To know of spirits till we hear
That voice, and see those eyes, fine Faye,
That lift our earthly lids halfway
Till into faery lands we peer.

Those eyes that beam the very light —
The hue that only flowers can bring:
That mouth, the honied murmuring
Of bees enamoured in their flight!
We listen, and we gaze, and fight
In vain against this lore you teach.
Because those faery lips that preach
Must feed on perfume day and night.

Alas for me who have been nursed
Ever with spirits (bad or good)!
'Twere hard if I not understood
The faintest whisper of their wings —
The scent which hints their presence first.
But ah! when some world-fetted calf
Wakens to first vague glimmerings
Of soul beneath your reasonings —
Then, Mab, I see your eyelids laugh!

As when the half-god Orpheus stood
Steeped to the soul in ecstasy
Of expectation strained to see,
What melody would do with wood.
I fancy how the harp-string stopt
Just as the trees began to prance;
Fancy the muttered words he dropt,
"I might have known that they would dance."

RENOVATION

It was a fervid Summer's eve;
And deep in Penge's woodbine bowers,
I walked to wear away the hours,
And snatch a short reprieve

From that unending coil the world
Kept dinning in mine ears and head:
And now the latest sun-glance red
The twilight sky impearled.

The blaze upon the forest spread

Was golden-misty, splendent-dead;
The sounds that in the wood were heard
Were those the ringdove and the bird

Of night and sorrow alternate
To any ear that listens late, —
Listens what nature doth alone
When men are sleep-o'erthrown.

I saw a Lady in the wood
Come watering every tree and herb.
And fixing such as winds disturb
With storm-blast over-rude.

She closed the cups of hundred flowers.
She held a starlight lantern dim
To those whose stalk is slight and slim
Throughout the silent hours.

She wakened mouse and hedgehog's sight,
Enkindled many a glow-worm spark.
And showed the mole in chamber dark
A transitory light;

Until a rustling stirring soon
Went through the leaves across the ground;
And listening silence pressed around
To pry into night's noon.

Myriads were moving and awake.
Myriads were moving to and fro;
Whisperings along the ground did go,
And grass and leaflets shake.

The stars were twinkling in and out:
The Lady ever with her hand
Tree, bush, herb, floweret, leaflet, fenned,
And showered their scents about.

Then from the holt my footsteps went
In wonder-silent shrinking awe;
For still where last I trod I saw
She raised the grass down bent.

And she caresses every blade,
And lifts up every floweret's head,
Whatever with unheedful tread
I trod on and God made.

IN THE GARDEN

If, when I lay me down to sleep,
This night I lose my wonted breath,
And pale and silent pass away
To some undreamed-of realm of death;

I wonder, love, if I would keep
Remembrance of this mortal sphere —
If that which is so dear to life
Would be to shadowy death as dear.

Could I not wed my faith with that,
To love you so were naught of bliss.
We soon shall know! Sit near me — here
We have not long to love and kiss!

You wear a rose-bud in your hair;
Is it the one you wore last June?
The moon comes with the sunset. Look!
It has the shape of last year's moon.

There 's no one coming, 'twas a bird
The same that swung on cherry boughs
Last year, and chirped and twittered so
About the garden and the house.

Hark how the marvellous music floats,
Beyond the elms by Arthur's Grange:
The bird is young, the song is old;
Shapes, but not spirits, suffer change.

What was I saying? Love shall last.
And never old and tarnished grow?
Dear heart, I think to those who love
All things in Nature promise so.

TO—

No word of question would I ask:
I would not learn in this dim world
Thy doom, or move aside the mask,
And find, as I have found before,

Beneath this flower the worm up-curled
That eats my flowers for evermore.

But now, before the ensanguined worm
That kills thy beauty leaves his nest;
And ere I probe the inward germ
And look down on a blinding blight —
Shall I be grudged an hour of rest,
An hour of rest in fate's despite?

To lie entranced and sing the songs
Appointed for the bower of God —
To drink the grandeur that belongs
To summer suns and golden moons —
The opiate languor roses nod
On the feint wind till he too swoons?

And that bemisted odour breathed
From golden-centred lilies? Deep
Now grows the charm; and interwreathed
With rings of radiance, lo, these brows
Are aching through a weight of sleep
Thy presence breathes among the boughs, —

Hanging on pendent bud and bell,
Charmed leaf, and fruit, and list'ning bird.
That dare not let its warble swell
Because the blank chasm widens round.
Engirding, till thy lips have stirred.
Silence, at watch for that sole sound.

Because the summer-bee will pause
Within the caetus' fulgid glare;
The wasp stand still in the hot air;
And down the deep white calla cup
There will not rise the soft applause
Until thou lift thine eyelids up.

So demons whisper woe in vain!
For I have neither ear nor sight.
I dream here on the edge of night;
Here where the calm cold ghosts have passed
A girdle round the placid plain
To hold the charmed sunset fast.

A WITCH OF RHINE

O get ye into the boat with me
For I am the witch of the winding Rhine —
And ye shall see
How sleepily
The lights that fly
Across the sky
Under the run of the river shine.

And ye shall see how winsomely
The flowers do grow beneath the river:
Marvel to see
What things they be
That grow so low
Where no winds blow,
And waters stream on, on for ever.

The stars are out, the stars are in.
The moon is here and there on the stream;
And let it glimmer
In sheen or dimmer.
There 's nothing ye
In the waters see
That 's half so empty as life's thin dream.

Lispeth and lappeth the wave on the boat,
For I am the witch of the winding Rhine,
I lived with you
In sun and dew.
Wind, ice, and snow,
And only know
There was nothing real in that life of mine.

Wherefore in — into the boat with me;
On the surface go and the current under.
And under and deeper
Where never a sleeper
(Who dreams more true
Than all of you)
Was wakened even by loudest thunder.

TARDY SPRING

O sun has earth no influence
To win thee back in time of spring?
And heed'st thou not the year's intense

Desire, the eager blossoming,
The yearning of the birds to sing
Bewrayed by this vain fluttering?

I hear the blackbird, and anon
The thrush — but oh their hearts are feint,
And there 's a chilly twitter on
The pear tree. 'Tis thy turn to paint
Some cloud with crimson now: the quaint
Spring pageant waits for thee alone.

I've walked the garden three times round.
Have questioned with the bustling ants,
And solitary bee that chants
A dismal drone — we cannot find
What keeps thee all so long behind;—
The seeds are swollen in the ground.

And cumbrous forms of life have changed
To comelier, demanding wings.
The secret motion of the Spring's
Desire anew hath atoms ranged,
And even now the whisperings
Of life pervade the germ of things.

That gold-striped snail I could but spare
A fortnight since for promising
The early coming of the spring,
Although he makes the gardens bare,
Hath closed his gummy shutters fast
Against this snowing eastern blast.

And were it not the faithful birds
Persist to say, O cruel sun.
That springtime must be — is begun,
I would believe, with snail, and herds
There sheltering beside the wall,
That we shall see no spring at all.

And, by some error unobserved
Before, December followeth
On April's heel, with winter-breath
To blow out all the golden lamps.
And starry flowers whose stems unnerved
Hang sidewise in the freezing damps-

I would believe; but that the thrush
Says resolutely still "the Spring!"

With faith so firm against this rush
Of winter wind that rocks him now,
That hoping spring, he dares to sing,
Without a leaf upon the bough.

And, if you listen, you shall hear
How he has clothed, in ecstasy.
With summer leaves each garden tree,
And brought a heated atmosphere
To that pale calm which keeps afloat
The thrillings of his evening throat.

Dear bird, (if thou art nothing more
Than what we see — a three years thing,)
With faith so firm thou canst defy
Thy present, and thy future sing
So gladly, I would fain that I
Had something of thy prophet lore:

For I am pined with sorrowing:
The present presses me so sore.
And of my future, less or more,
I cannot augur anything
With thy large faith, but beat the floor
Of hopeless human reasoning.

A WOMAN'S BEAUTY

Not any fragrance blown from flowers,
Not any growth of summer hours,
Nor all the whispers of the sea.
Kissed by relenting winds;
Nor that thrilled bliss the mountain finds
By Dian nightly visited; —
Only the rapture of the dead.
Voyaging the unvoyaged sea
To its mysterious shore, may be
The rapture that thy beauty breeds in me.

Death-craving stars that passionately
Burn and die,
And they that listen
The music of the amethystine
Turning heavens eternally.
Are all too ardent or too cold —
For lo, thy beauty, like the radiance rolled

Out of yon closing sunset gates of gold.
Rains soft upon the spirit and wraps it fold in fold.

O lady, what is this thou art on earth?
A vision of the unvexed world, a dream
Of the eternal peace, where sorrow and sin
And failure, and the aching spirit's dearth
No more will enter in?
Yea, thou art mocking us — before the time
Tormenting us — a cruel clearest gleam
Of heaven too high to climb!

Or rather is it, this world sleepy grown,
And cumbered in sciential self-conceit.
Needs a reminder of forgotten love?
Wherefore thou with gentle feet
Hast journeyed here in person of love's own
Sweet spirit to reprove.
The nightingale hath fled into the grove,
The skylark telleth to the Minting stars
What no brain dreameth of.
The lily breathes her joy. And yet ye groan
Within your prison-bars
Of knowledge, whereas love may here be seen and known.

A GOOD-BYE

Come a little way on the lea, Mary.
Let us, at least, say our good-bye;
That fervid gaze of fire that burns the west
Turns to the cold star in the sky.

The merle and the mavis lingering
With music till the daylight die.
And small birds weary with sleepy eye that sing.
Grudge not the time for their good-bye.

IDOLS

The clouds are heaped: the winds have blown
The wandering flock in a fleecy sea.
And left clear space for the moon, alone
Descending to the level lea
Where stands a black rude Rocking Stone.

In her clear path circling down,
Growing broader gradually,
Staring on the level lea.
Standing on the Rocking Stone;
She shall sink down suddenly.
Yet she pauses drowsily —
A final linger ere she fall:
Hearken now the clear wind call!
To the bare wolds calleth he:
The moon hears not his song.
For a giant lies along.
Sleeping in the shadow, rocking
Like one sleeping, but the mocking
Moon says he will not awake
As of old his thirst to slake.
Musing yet upon this stone?
Can she even see the stain
Of what he will not drink again —
Is it not his elbow-bone
She slideth down?
Was the giant arm upthrown
In his first sleep; does he never
More unbend it, rocking ever?
Circling him with golden ring
She answers, "Once a king."
The moon knows what a god he was.
And she knows how deadly deep
He lieth in petrific sleep:
And she knows each god that has
Slept since his time, and count will take
Of other gods of rarer make:
These gods of vapour, and of gas.
And lightning, these that lure the mass
To worship them, that spout and shake
Their periods, and pass.

AN EPIDEMIC

I heard the wheel that clattered still.
And on the common where I stood
Was little sign of human ill,
Nor hint that pestilence could brood
Where shadows wrapped the distant wood.

And many a white-faced village post
That here and there, with chain between.

Gave stir of life to all the green.
Said nothing of the hearse that crossed
A while ago. And you had been

Persuaded all the village throve
In life and health, and that the trees
Which stand so stately in the grove
Were fanned by no dead airs that seize
At midnight on pale mouths we love.

I had been reading, half the day.
Of wondrous change by science wrought:
But here the children seemed to play
As hitherto, and art had brought
No sweetness to the blackbird's lay;

Nor any solemn-suited thought
To infants who would play no more
A bow-shot from the accustomed door
Because a mother's life was not.
And nature moved as heretofore.

LIGHTS AND SHADOWS

Ho! singing high on the hill,
Ah! singing under the vale.
Fleet sun and shadow
Move over the meadow,
Nothing abiding still;
The cattle, cloud, wind-moving:
A laughing on hill and in gale,
A voice in the valley reproving
And laughing and loving at shepherds' will.

Sing me, you thrush in the elm,
A single song and stay;
The song-waves overwhelm.
Over the meadows all day
Move sun and shadow — nay.
Rest, rest!
There is aching in the breast
Whatever idle shepherds say.

And the perdurable green
Of holly, and the running river.
And the ash that holds its mast,

Will they last?
When we have passed, and shiver

In the wood's serene,
Whose branches dream and grieve?
Whereof it were not good
Ye shepherds understood,
Dreaming on November eve.

ALIENS

Love, when I meet thee face to face,
I feel thou art not of my race;
I know thy language is not mine,
Or only so in the hollow sign
The lips make. Of my world of things
Thou hast no care or questionings,
Nor I of thine.

What words are said between us twain
I strive to recollect, in vain.
Such merest sounds the words we say,
Our souls might be in separate spheres
That own another night and day;
Thy smile, God knows, may count for tears!

And with thy smile, and with thy sighs,
A subtle effluence of thine eyes.
And a dim woven atmosphere
Around me when thy voice is near.
My spirit is taken swooning-wise
As death would take it, swathed in sleep.
Fatal enchantress, take thy spell.
Spell passion-deep
From off me, for I love not thee —
I know thee not — thy heart can tell
Thou know'st not me.

What converse can be ours this way?
More natural to sit dumb and stare,
As two strange creatures, wondering, glare
Each upon each in silent fear,
Conjeduring what keen weapons they
Conceal to poison, crush or tear —
Conceal to unsheathe but once, and slay.

"Wherefore," I said, "no hope within my heart
Where hate was dead and sorrow laid asleep?
Wherefore," I said, "play out thy sorry part,
Neither to laugh nor weep?

"Arming for ever with no foe to fight.
And girding up thy loins where goal is none,
Or making for the goal of final night
Wherein no work is done."

Yea then (as if a word could cheer the sight)
I knew thee and I said at last: " The song
Wherewith I hailed my morning doth belong
To none but thee, O Night!

"Is due at last to thee, strange speechless Night!
Thee who hast followed me with faithful feet.
To be mine own, my mistress sole and sweet.
Knowing me thine of right.

"Well laugh'st thou, who didst know me fi-om the first
A thriftless wanderer on the sunny ways —
Through all the heat and strife of long-drawn days.
And strain and toil and thirst.

"When I stood still, as one who having spied
A light of water springs, on nearing it
Finds shining rushes in the moon-flame lit,
But dusty all and dried.

"And didst thou see my heart in its delight
Counting on ease at last and holidays.
And building labyrinths with pleasant ways?
And didst thou smile, O Night,

"Knowing how soon thy truant would return
With festal torches dipt in funeral gloom.
And birthdays bearing dates of death and doom?
All this didst thou discern,

"But bodest waiting for me all the same.
Letting me taste and weary of the light,
And taking me at last with tears of shame
Which thou wilt dry, O Night!

"Content thee if I weave my crown aright,
A dainty faultless-fitting cypress wreath.
That grew in the charmed darkness underneath
Thy tresses, noiseless Night.

"And tell me, queen, how we may live together
Now all the vain pursuit of light has ended:
What deep-wrought haven for thy last-befriended
Waits in the stormless weather.

"What glimmering mountains, what dim ghosts of trees?
Whisper in thy most calm and quiet breath,
As calm but scarcely quite so cold as death,
Unfold thy realms of peace.

"Dark, yea, for thou art Darkness' queen, I know,
And imageless, — save what dim imagery
Around the spirit dreaming nakedly
In phosphor gleam doth glow.

"So in thy secret arms, encircling Night,
Communing close, without restraint or bar.
Absolved from fret of sun or moon or star.
Beyond all gaze of light,

"I have essayed to rest me while the spheres
Roll round in anguish, and we dream of peace.
But, O divinest mistress, what be these
Phantoms of hopes or fears?

"What portraiture up-growing in the gloom?
What eyes like stars that burn through moonless skies?
What mouth the black-red peony petal dyes?
What hair of raven's plume?"

And lo, obscurest dream or lucid dream
(Out of the darkness woven and the clime
Of death, but all untouched by death or time
The soul's self-kindled beam.

Growing to more than mundane permanence
Of vital verity as pored upon
By form-engendering spirit) to thought puts on
Its outmost evidence.

Even as the slow-resolving plants supply
A foodful soil whereon new growths are fed,

So the spent thought its pristine form will shed
Fresh thought to vivify;

Or as a man left on a lonely isle
Hath sometimes spoken aloud to hear the sound
Of his own voice, and listening hath found
Words lost to him erewhile;

Even so the spirit spins from subtlest thread
New robes in which she wraps her with delight.
No form of earth or heaven will fester dead
In these thy courts, O Night

And here will blossom every flowret sweet.
And every carol of the blithest bird
I hear in springtime will again be heard
No more to fade or fleet.

Only thou sayest, thou art darkness all.
And I — am I not weary of the light?
What hand is painting on thy lifeless pall
These forms of life, O Night?

A THRUSH'S SONG

What, sitting in the underwood, I heard —
If I should tell it now, who would believe?
Not thou, my Annie! But the wind will weave
Words in his own song-tissue till the bird
Sings more than notes to me, when not a third
Hearer participates the summer's eve —
Oh the wood hearkens when her children grieve!
Wilt listen? I will tell thee word for word.

Only this human harp must change its strings
To take the tone of sylvan minstrelsy,
And we must couple to our fancy wings
Who mean to hear the depth and mystery
Of what within my ear still plains and rings —
The burden of the thrush's threnody.

"Sweet! Sweet! Sweet!"
So I sang, and so
She seemed to listen.
Then I said, " Sing low.
Sun, these stars will glisten.

Let summer come or summer go."

I sang, "Be quick! Be quick!"
But then she said, "No, no."
She would not listen.
Then I sang, "What though
The night make speed to go,
The morrow's sun to glow,
Will mine be risen?
Let winter come, let summer go."

I sang, "Alight, alight!"
The morning drove the night
Westward, and hung the high boughs all with dew;
To these or those she flew, —
The starry eyes of dew!
If she listened
I know not, and the starry droplets glistened.
I sang, "Alight, alight! " from my dark yew;
If she did listen
I never knew.
I sang, "Alight, alight! "from this dark yew;
If she could listen
I shall not know.
I sang, "Alight, alight!" until the night
I sang, "Let night come now and never go."

SKYLARKS

The larks sang gay in Long Law-ford:
The sky was ruddy at even;
Each day had heard as cruel a wind
As ever sang through heaven.
' How many a day
Will the mad wind stay?"
I heard her say, on the dusty way, —
Overhead the larks sang gay.

The larks sang gay in Long Law-ford
Even to the set of sun:
And I saw dip a cloud-built ship
Whose masts snapt one by one.
It bred in me
Thought silently:
"This girl she knows of a ship at sea," —
Down the last lark dropt on the lea.

The larks sing gay in Long Law-ford
All day to the fell of dew:
For what they sing, a God-given thing.
Is joy the summer through.
So gaily they sing: but to me never ring
The notes of their joy-rhyme true.
Since I heard that maiden rue.

IN A WOOD

O Lady, deign with me to walk,
Awhile to walk within the wood;
What thrushes sing and turtles brood
To hearken while the dim walks strew'd
With whispering leaves we trace and talk.

Ah, Lady, had you seen the wood,
And seen the secret conscious sky
Beyond the beechen branchery
So calm yestreen at sunset brood
Before the crows began to cry!

And in the wood are mysteries,
Unchanted songs, that float away
Off solid solemn cypresses,
A something from where nothing is:
No birds are sitting on the spray.

The blossoms flash in yellow flames.
They glimmer in a purple glow;
They wake in all the woods below
Occulted flowers that find no names
With men — so quick they bloom and go.

Few footsteps on these paths intrude!
A spirit of fear through all its boughs
Defends our charmed forest house,
That musing owls may dream and drowse,
And hares sleep safely unpursued.

The stars have spaces in the wood
Wherein they circle dreamily
All the night long till bat and bee
Cross in flight, when, day renewed.
The star-dance ceases suddenly.

But when the gold-disked daylight stood.
Stood gazing ere he went away,
I heard a strange sweet singing say.
Say and repeat it (were it good
That I repeat such song to-day?

He sang it soothly yesterday.)
"The wood is growing dark," he said.
He said, " the gloom begins to grow:
Come quickly, night, and quickly go.
To-morrow all the past is dead.

"To-morrow comes a queenly maid.
The maid our minstrel pines to know;
Come quickly, night, and quickly go.
For neither have the stars delayed.
And silence wills to have it so."

Hearken the wonders of the wood:
The thrushes have a quainter throat.
The blackbird has a bolder note,
The squirrel has a softer coat,
The oak tree has a grander mood.

Lady, will you scorn the wood?
Ah, Lady, will you say me nay?
And that true bird did promise yea.
And I have trusted long and woo'd
Your shadow through the morning grey.

And at the hour of waning day
Two turtles colloquied the same.
Ah, Lady, is my heart to blame?
I dreamed the sun was dropt away.
And all the world a burning flame.

Nay, Lady, what is this you say.
You are no substance but of air?
But, Lady, this is all my care.
That in the wood these limbs I lay,
So we may walk together there.

A NIGHT LAY

Hate and love and hope and fear,

Never more to enter here,
O night!
Thou saw'st the sorry race was run:
In the dim
Thou saw'st me swim —
How I strove and how I won
In the sun.
Then how I learned to loathe the light,
O night!
Thou my Queen, my loveliest.
Thy domain is rest.
Is there anything to see
In thy house of ebony?
Surely overhang thy house
Cypress boughs:
As calm but scarce so cold as death
Is thy breath.

FORGET ME NOT

I will not say, "Forget me not"
To you.
For if it means true friends are true
For ever, as the freshet's brink
Is to the sky.
Shall I
Tell you of whom to think?
Or say "Forget me not" —
For what?

CRIME'S BLIGHT

The dell was deep and darkly screened,
Over its brink the maple leaned,
And in its sides grew larch and thorn.
And ash upreared to greet the morn —
Morn which ne'er glimmered on the grass —
And nettles down the dell. You pass
There as a place meant to be passed.
Not visited. But when, at last.
Chance, fete, or what you will, had taught
My feet to stay here, I was caught
Strangely as in a magic net
(Like one foredoomed whose task is set)

To where the bare roots writhe and twine
In dragonish fashion; it was mine
To lie, and dream and strive to unbind
The shrouded mystery enshrined
In these dark boughs. For you could know,
Having once sat there, it was so:
Some deed done here by man or heaven
Or hell, in years long gone, had given
A touch of shivering to the place.
And if you looked your eye could trace
A track beneath the trees where grew
No grass nor any herb, where dew
Fell not, nor summer shower, a track
Half round the dell, barren and black.
From east to west in crescent-wise
It goes, as you look up the rise:
You see where the dark line begins;
But be it sorrow's mark or sin's,
All else is fair. Not lovelier
Grows maple, hawthorn, ash, or fir.
Than there, when springtime breathings stir,
Or summer hears the grasshopper.
The guilt is in the blighted ground
Alone, and if these trees have found
A somewhat melancholy mood.
Believe 'tis where the branches brood
Over that black and baleful earth;
And if the birds withhold their mirth.
Believe 'tis from these lowest boughs
Alone, left to the dull carouse
Of bat and beetle and wood-louse.

SEPARATION

"When will she come?"
Night by night and day by day,
Sore at heart, I sigh and say.
"Where lies my home?"
Seven weeks ago this way it lay,
And yet I cannot find my way.
"Is this the sun?"
Sore at heart I sigh and say,
Cold is the sun, my love away.
"The day is done,"
Sore of heart I sigh and say.
The night is drear and drear the day.

SEASIDE

O Annie, if your hand could be
Within my hand beside the sea.
With sky, and sea, and sunny mist,
In sapphire and in amethyst.
Dreaming their early morning dream.
As from the Cliff's head it did seem
The morn I left. If we could stand
Beside that sea-wall, hand in hand!

The sea-wall there is tawny sand.
Brown, yellow, rough with broom and gorse,
And little water-runnels course
Their way down to the tide-washed strand.
Where we have seen them fade, as if
The spirit of their native cliff,
Jealous of ocean's briny reign.
Had sucked them back through earth again.

And, Annie, when the noon is clear,
Have we not watched upon the wave
The sea-birds sitting, — lost in grave
Conjecture how their seat could be
So firm upon the moving sea?

Love, you remember this, and more;
And how we wandered up the shore
With our bold boy, in search of shells.
To where the bright spa-water wells.

Ah, love, I dare not muse on those
Dull, drooping hours which followed close
That noonday walk, but rather dwell
On minutes stol'n, while he slept well.
When we would nimbly thrid the town,
With all its evening shadows brown.
Till, in the starry blackness, we
Came out upon the rushing sea.

Then the walk home, in converse low.
Of what is given to few to know.
Nature's own words of light and shade
That yellow sands and pine trees made
At sunset, for no eye but ours.

The mystery of the cloud-built towers,
Mute music of green moss and flowers.
And magic morn and evening hours.

These things we talked of, O my sweet! —
Do you, who see them now, repeat
The old words, as I do, leagues away?
Or will you chide me if I say
(For your own silent secret ear)
Some presence must have touched more near
Than Nature's even — or else why prove
Thy words more blissful, O my love?

A QUIET EVENING

From mere ennui the very cat
Walked out — it was so precious flat.
Due on the sofa Gabriel sat.
And next to him was Stephens found;
I think, but am not certain, that
The fender William's legs were round.

However, all was drowsy, mild.
And nothing like to break the charm.
Though John essayed in some alarm
To read his latest muse-born child;
Then Gabriel moved his active arm.
And some believe that Stephens smiled.

But certain 'tis that Aleck, who
Had watched that arm, as anglers do
Their quiet float, an hour or two.
Was pleased to find it move at last.
He therefore filled his pipe anew.
And doubled the mundungus blast.

The poem yet went on and on:
The poet kept his eyes upon
The paper till the piece was done;
And then the coke-fire's roof fell in.
Another accident, which one
Should mention, William scorched his shin.

And nothing more till supper time:
Except that Gabriel read a rhyme
Of Hell and Heaven and ghosts and crime

That gave the room a kind of chill,
And rapture followed — so sublime
That forty minutes all was still.

Till all the solemn company
Went down to supper — verily
The supper went off quietly.
Trying to talk was all in vain:
And then we went up silently
Into the lonesome room again.

Oh was it quiet? I can swear
I heard the separate gas lights flare,
The creak of the vibrating chair
The balanced Aleck swung upon:
The balanced Aleck swinging there
Knew it, and so went swinging on.

Six men, each seated in his seat.
With body, arms, and legs complete—
A passive mass of flesh, alack!
That none but human cattle make!
The wonder was that they could meet
So silent and so long awake.

But Gabriel coiled himself, at last.
Upon the sofa — Stephens cast
His weary arms out, William past
A thoughtful hand across his eyes.
And George has blown a fainter blast
To listen till the snores arise.

And somewhat quickly they arose —
He could distinguish Gabriel's nose
From William's mouth in sweet repose.
Whose measured murmurs now began;
While John L. Tupper, half in dose.
Was crooning as he only can.

And Stephens — no, he took to flight
Before he slept. Then Aleck's sight
Denied his pipe was yet alight;
He put it down and grimly stared.
Then crammed it to the muzzle tight.
And listened — that was all he dared.

For not a waking P. R. B.
Was left; a blinding mystery

Of smoke was over all the three
Enduring souls that kept awake.
They listened — ^'twas the harmony
Of cats! — or there was some mistake.

Then looking on the garden plot
Without, they verified the not
Unwelcome feet: the cats had got
Convivial, sure enough; and we
Could recognize friend Thomas hot
In mirth like Burns " among the three."

But if the cats held conference,
What then? We might not make pretence
To such — witness the prudent sense
Of Stephens getting up to go.
I'd give my cat the preference.
Who left us somewhat sooner, though.

PROGRESS OF THE SPECIES

You're sanguine, very sanguine, a good sign
You have discovered an invisible power
That runs along your wires around the world
Called electricity — the word is much.
Then comes another invisible in your pipes
To nullify the night, — gas. Call it so,
The visible candle is a vulgar thing!
That handy artist light who flits about
Ready, at beck, to paint your visages.
What name will ye be pleased to accost him by?
John, James, were scarce distingue let him be
Photography.
Dear man, you must have hated tangibles.
Push further yet — the chairs and table dance
By simple touching. You must look, nay, think
These into physical obedience. Call
The chair you wish to sit on to your side.
And these are dead trees, do you understand.
The dead ones of your kin. Be sure, they'll come
(Hailed by a potent over-mastering will)
In terrible haste— all the old mouldy sticks,
Kepler and Newton, Tycho, Verulam,
To knock out lame excuses in your ears
For their lugubrious existences.

Oh we'll have such a rout of them! But you
Go on — stagnation's death, only hold fast
On galvanism, and mesmerism, and steam,
And gas, and anaesthetics! . . . How d'ye do.
My dearest Smith? you see I know a bare
Truth — your euphonious patronymic.

[Smith.] "Ha!"
"Why, what in Mammon's name can bring you here?
Are you lichen hunting, out for orchids — cut
Grey ledgers for a green day in the woods? "
[Smith.] "No, I'm going to the Palace. Pretty well?"
" Excellent, excellent! such an appetite!
I dine directly — won't you stay? "

[Smith.] "How? where?"
"Here, just by."

[Smith.] "In the wood?" "There, Smith, behold
My restaurant. This host of mine so shifts
His tables, I have no monotony
Of scene while feasting, look you, to keep pace
With keen requirements of this ultimate age.
This last perfection of the toiling world.
I choose to balance well the dignities
That decorate this human microcosm;
To give the bodily ministers — the gross
Slaves of the mind — their grosser nutriment;
But not, while these are glutted (far, so far
Below in their material house), to have
Their supreme lord, the spirit, intoxicate.
Or sleeping on his throne. The Romans built
Baths high into the air, that while they swam.
Ridding their bodies of gross scale and slough.
And drinking in the purer lymph, their eyes
Might wander far along the coasts below.
And feed their minds with thought, or greet the dawn
Through slumbrous floods of summer-purple night;
For we must dip back into Rome and Greece,
For fear we miss some handy requisite.
Just as our traveller in Naples says.
Who, having thridded Herculaneum,
Pompeii, and the obvious treasure-heaps.
Must look well to the guide book lest he miss
What 's underneath the house he lodges in, —
A catacomb with cinerary urns.
And tell me, is it fair, my sapient Smith,
To cheat the nineteenth century microcosm

One atom of accumulated wealth?
Or, whilst you harbour galvanism and steam
As household slaves discreetly ministrant.
To so, so far forget your grosser needs.
As, if you wanted hazel-kernels, now
To rush into the wood and gobble down
The hazel leaves and all? What folly then
Is here! we know — blest science teaches us —
The stomach craves matter to triturate;
The lacteal glands, albumen; and so forth.
Inside the wood 's a certain bark, my friend:
Moistened or dry, 'twill serve the stomach well
For grinding purposes. Albumen next,
And olein for the lacteals — look there!
Creeping so slowly, turning every view
To tempt a man, the partridge has his leave
To whirr away — we'll not go after him.
The long slow slug cased o'er with silver light,
(What 's meant for man is well within his reach,)
Two coloured spiral snails that seem to screw
Into the craving appetite — these have
Excess of the nutritious element,
Minus the fibre of the barbarous ox.
See — covers laid for two — observe both shells,
What elegant ornamental cookery!
The Romans didn't shut their eyes to this —
Even the shell has nutrient properties —
The crust of a raised pie. You'll stop and dine?"
"I thank you, thanks, but appetite won't serve
So early in the day as this with me.
You see my office keeps me on till four.
And then, when I get home, I have to dress."

A GROTESQUE

RURAL SOUNDS

(Morning)

The pigs are whistling on the hill,
The cart-horse singeth blithe,
The crows are tinkling feint and shrill,
The fox-glove wets his scythe;
And shall we linger slumbering still
While such sweet sounds are rife?
Oh quit thy slothful window-sill.

And plunge into the strife.

SOCIAL SOUNDS

(Noon)

Hark to the bobby's bounce and buzz.
And this hot pavement's hum:
As jocund as the Man of Uz
Singeth the East end slum.
Oh were it not a bitter thought.
To live and never die.
How cheerfully (but dearly bought)
Such sounds might meet the eye!

SOLEMN SOUNDS

(Night)

Where ocean stays his warbling flight,
And rocks no further roam,
But listen midst the glare of night,
The yellow, sounding foam;
No minstrelsy is half so sweet.
No perfume half so gay:
The lips are dazzled, and the feet
Of watch-dogs melt away.

CIRCUMSTANCES ALTER CASES

That last gust must have blown away the gable.
The chimney-pots, or something. To depart
Were safest now — and here goes for a start:
Not that I wish it, but because I'm able
Just now. This bedroom may be in the stable
A minute hence, and I have not the heart
To stand my ground, and own (however tart
Your sarcasm) I hold, it just a fable
That men are best-wise by experience taught.
Unless that soundest maxim you select
From interesting facts that are not fraught
With fatal consequences — You detect
My meaning doubtless. Make a grand onslaught
On turkeys, and be certain you'll be pecked.

BROWNING'S "SORDELLO"

"Sordello" I confess has puzzled me,
And I have read it — some will never read;
But go on to their end, like dogs indeed
Feeding and snarling almost equally:
But, that such tykes have just capacity
To value nobly that on which they feed,
Loathing Sordello, is not quite agreed —
We doubt they judge ev'n horse flesh righteously.

If ever any man should cut my throat,
I should be anxious, ere they hanged the knave.
That the phrenologists should ascertain
Whether his brain had ventricle or moat
Wherein perchance Sordello might have lain;
Demonstrate that, and I the man would save.

THE ONE THING KNOWN

Easy to say "there 's nothing that we know,"
But do we really know this If we do,
'Tis surely something, and the first 's not true.
We know, it seems, our knowledge does not go
Beyond the knowing this same knowledge so
Contracted that we have not mastered two
Truths yet; and then — after so long ado —
One empty truth is all we have to show.

A positive negative, but something yet:
Short men a long way off of being tall!
Income of poverty vast and secure!
Courage, O mortals! see the over-set
Of abstract doubt achieved, and, spite of all
The destinies, be sure you are not sure.

THE DEBIT SIDE

When whoso merely hath a little grain
Of faith, will keep that faith that is in him,
Not running after others for a whim.
Not keeping true men waiting in the rain:
When whoso keeps a covenant (on pain

Of pocket) from respect to custom trim.
Or some idea of honour very dim.
Or even from the dirty one of gain:
Be not too keen to cry, "So this is all —
A thing I might myself have done as well.
But would not do it for it was not worth."
Ask, is this fair? For is it still to tell
That of all blessed nuisances on earth.
The worst is waiting, quizzed by great and small?

THINGS UNPERCEIVED AND USES UNDISCERNED

A slow moon lifteth out her luculent horn
Above the umbrage: steering through the pines
She looks slant downward through the shafted lines
Of shadow, brightening bramble, sharpening thorn,
And forked toadstool, to where mists are born
At bottom of the dell: there sleeps she; shines
There broodingly among the eglantines,
Leaving the hillside utterly forlorn.
So seems it. But to one who climbs the hill
Slant-darkling through the thorny hanging ground.
Weak creeping lanterns glimmer green and chill.
There for a purpose will the dew drip round.
Holding nocturnal converse without sound.
And something through the grass at periods thrill.

TO MY FRIEND HOLMAN HUNT

I see so much of sorrow on the earth,
O Hunt, that — were it not for natural things.
The careless loitering of lucent springs.
The evening sweetness, and the morning mirth
Of songsters, and (far most, amidst this dearth
Of earthly love) thy brave endeavourings
To catch the far harmonious murmurings
That tell how calm a region gave them birth, —
I might be led to doubt, in evil hour,
(With such a failure as the world doth seem,
Where love and ruth front churlishness and hate) —
I might be won in darkened hour to dream
Of chance misrule, or evil guiding power,
But for these counsellings to hope and wait.

TO FREDERIC STEPHENS

Stephens, although you worked with heart and soul
And hand, to compass what has now been wrought;
And thought for others when was need of thought.
And comforted when weary weakness stole
On other workers — sharing half the dole;
Now that the labour to an end is brought.
The victors blazoned and the battle fought,
I do not read you on the popular roll

Much comfort! other work demands your hand.
God shall appoint a day when you will bear
Your own peculiar fruit. For it was planned
That these should no part of your guerdon share,
Toiling for others. God gave that command.
And wills that He give all the guerdon there.

MY DREAM

I

My mother, is it even two months to-day?
Like very truth, it seemed now I stood near
This window — with the bird's song at mine ear —
Moulding some fancied form in plastic clay;
Which suddenly began to sink away
Under my fingers, holding it in fear,
But that a voice came from the lawn as clear
As thrushes thrill the sinking sun to stay.
The voice cried, "Wait, I'll come." A voice no less
Moved by the mouth than was the heart in pain
To help me. So I watched the door for you, —
Which opened not. And soon the ghastly guess
That some grim gulph had rolled between us twain.
Grew into waking knowledge. And I knew.

II

No wonder when I call upon thy name
I hear no low reply to comfort me:
No wonder doubt endures eternally
Around the dwelling of the dead, and flame

Of fervid love burns dim beyond the frame
Of our terrene: no wonder fitfully
I catch the far-off tone of memory,
And know not through which gate the tidings came;
For so my world of sleep derives a power
Wanting whilom, and fashions thee more clear
Than daylight memory; and I believe
Thy visit actual at the midnight hour:
Without which solace, O companion dear,
A woeful life were mine, who wake and grieve.

UNACHIEVED

Love's triumph this! I would not have her sigh,
Nor hear her fine voice falter which is keen
And sweet as falling water heard between
Steep rocks in summer. My extremity
Of passion should not weigh upon her eye
And blanch her hue; and she should walk serene.
And pass me by, an inaccessible queen;
And I should offer her idolatry.

For, so, there comes, at least, no emptiness
Of heart and spirit. All the sorrow and teen,
And far-off hopeless hope, will last — will last:
My once clear moon will not wane lustreless;
Its glory never shall be overpast;
Unreached, it still must be what it has been.

AN EVENING FANTASY

But if you linger near to even-song,
When the calm flood of twilight overwhelms,
And hear the drone of wind pass down the elms.
And watch the night draw nearer to the long
Horizon's bend, until the belfry's tongue
Awake you: then unbar ambiguous realms
Of rock and lake, where barques with magic helms
Pursue their windless way bright isles among.
Pray Heaven you wake not in that forest land
Whose former cheerful glimpse of town and spire
Is banished by the baffling gloom, or stand
To feel the guilty trunks still winding higher.
And (while the spirits in bonds pant and suspire)

Clicking their dragon rind beneath your hand.

KIT'S COTTY-HOUSE, KENT

This autumn wanes — the day is ebbing out.
Upon the round of a bare, stubbly hill,
Four rugged stones are standing huge and still
And black against the west. Round, round about
I walk betwixt two spirits, wonder and doubt.
Pondering this witness to the invincible will;
Until I know the tyrant Time can kill
No purpose, where the heart is true and stout.
While lo and look you! moving round again.
What a weird misty moon is rising! Late
The night and year grow. Garnered is the grain;
All that can die is arming desperate
To brave the binding winter's straitening chain:
While these throughout all seasons "stand and wait."

TWILIGHT

I walked within the vine-clad garden wall
At even hush, as moonlight came to aid
The waning day: and while the day decayed.
Faint shade, that solely on white flowers would fell.
Followed me; till I thought — Indeed we call
This interval of neither shine nor shade
Nor sleep nor toil "twilight." Yet who essayed
To name a thing so unsubstantial?
For, wisdom, with thy boundaries limiting
God's creatures here, art thou not foolishness-
Naming far points and knowing merely these?
What is the thing and what the nothingness?
What all this labouring change from clouds to trees.
Through light to dark, beginning, vanishing?

A THRUSH'S MESSAGE

What might it mean? The thrush at eventide
When the red sun was lingering on the line
Where frozen earth and glowing sky combine,
Sang as if less to sing than speak he tried.

For oh to me, " Be quick!" it seemed he cried.
To me whom, waiting for a fond design
To be fulfilled (if Heaven my way incline).
Some hope now near my sunset has espied.

"Be quick! Be quick!" Alas, amen, said I.
Is it thy mate thou callest to thy nest?
Or dost thou to the woodland muses cry,
To bring thee thy full throat? or wouldst thou wrest
Some touch of magic beauty unpossessed
By other sunsets from this sanguine sky?

OF SUCH IS THE KINGDOM OF HEAVEN

The lovingness of souls must needs be great
When they have moulted off their vain disguise,
If we dare picture them in any wise
From children, newly entering on our state
Of wonder, having not yet learned to hate.
Or hide the love they carry in their eyes,
Or look unfaithful passion, that belies
The heart, to leave it scarred and obdurate.

Alas alas! would all of us be glad
To enter in Christ's kingdom where the folk
Are such as these? We surely should repine,
And sigh for old disguises — grown so mad
That God's true heaven would seem an arduous yoke
If age first grew not meek and infantine.

RAIN

After a thirsting summer came the rain,
Laggard, unwelcome at September's end;
But, as one dying revives to know his friend.
The faint earth brightened and looked green again:
And I, who walked and watched the daylight wane,
And saw the wet clouds silently descend.
And the half-famished sheep where they were penned.
Said "Surely this comes mockingly in vain!"
"Vain? " laughed an echo: "Shrunken brooks are filling;
Some bird's throat opens thankfully between
This light and dark; some weeds say. We are willing
Again before the winter to be green;

Some newt's ear hearkens to the drops distilling.
Are thy delights all that the angels mean?"

RUE TRONCHET, PARIS

When wind was fresh at morn, and early sun
Smote the top story of the high-built street.
And these roof-shadows sprang across to greet
The windows opposite, half walk, half run
(So light this air of Paris maketh one)
I went; and not with the old grave, discreet.
Staid step — it is a charm, it is a cheat
That wins — and no one knows till he is won.
Even so! Then to a place where fountains play
I came, and saw a solemn obelisk.
Graven with dynasties long fallen away.
Climb up the morning. Here the Frenchmen frisk.
And fountains spurt, and bubbles burst to spray
Round Egypt's granite — time's blank asterisk!

TO THE CUCKOO

If, cuckoo, it bodes any good in love
To hear thy note after the nightingale,
Little, alas, for him should it avail
Whose hair is growing scant and grey above
His temples: little profits he thereof:
Therefore thou leavest me, alone to hail
The bird of love who now thou know'st would fail
To bring me any help in wood or grove.
So hold'st thou up a mirror for my life,
Despiteful bird that grudgest me my gains.
Me who have little sorrow that 'tis so.
So have I dreamed of calm 'mid storm and strife.
And I have mused of mountains in the plains.
And I have sung of summer in the snow.

TO A SKYLARK

O fervid poet, chanting even and morn,
Who so ador'st the sun thou dost not tire
Singing for aye his glory to the higher

Regions I may not reach, a thought forlorn
Hath seized me, that thou own'st a love inborn
I know not, nor can know, though I aspire
In spirit to thy constant quenchless fire
Which, save one idol, all things seems to scorn.
For neither sun nor star nor witching moon
Can hold me long, but still my heart doth rove,
Seeking for ever some unknown delight:
Beauty in man or woman cannot smite
My heart so deep but still a new-found love
Enchants it to be disenchanted soon.

SUB JOVE

After a day of heat at end of June,
While the last rain mist swathed the lawns in white,
And when no breath of wind breathed on the night.
There rolled along the heaven a magic moon.
My spirit spoke, "Lest ye be home too soon
For sleep, stay here, and turn your bodily sight
On earth and sky, dreaming in silent night
Of all that will be done by morrow-morn."
Then did I yearn in that thrice charmed hour.
Dream with the dreaming trees, glow with the stars
That feint in odour and drip cold in dew;
Yet never gained I glimpse of all the power
Behind the five insuperable bars,
Who held me swooning till the first cock crew.

TO A NIGHTINGALE

O Nightingale, that singest till the dawn
Through all the starry changes of the nighty
Wasting thy passionate heart with fervid might.
The sun is sunk away and the day gone:
Now unto what dark sanctuary withdrawn,
Beyond the reach of peevish sound and sight,
Pourest thou forth such wild and wild delight.
And sittest thrilling this dim moon-lit lawn?

Triumph of song thou pauseless dost outpour
By thy great faith in the great stress of love.
That moves the worlds to music as of yore;
Now the night creepeth down with yearning sore

At heart of silence — meadow and wood and grove.
And bending moon and listening stars approve.

IF I KNEW!

Ah if I knew that thy divinest eyes
Had read the story of my heart's heart-love,
Knowing (what little profits me to know)
That neither sleep nor night nor dim remove
Avails to quench their fire that, like moonrise.
Rose on my ravished spirit a year ago!
How all my hope is like a lamp gone low.
And all my heart burnt out in ecstasies!
Only the knowing this were known to thee
Would make some tide of life-blood to renew
My heart, and some sweet hope come back to me.
The lonely realms of paradisal dew.
The golden isles within the enchanted sea
Were not so far to voyage. Ah if I knew!

WOMEN'S RIGHTS

Now know I well this nation's strength doth wane.
But not because its eager intellect:
Hath taken means for end, losing respect:
Of self, industrious (in a miser's vein)
To heap up ever what is counted gain,
Much too intent on hoarding to detect:
If that be gain or no. Even this defeat.
This trick of mind might right itself, with strain.
But when I see our heart of woman turned
To worship in this wise, her brow engrossed
And hardened with a weight of wisdom earned
At such an impious and unnatural cost.
Her dower of beauty dim and undiscerned: —
Then know I that the land I loved is lost.

TO ANNIE

Annie, if any verse of mine might win
The obdurate heart of Time to let it live,
When I am mingled with the fugitive

Fleet elements wherein all lives begin
And end: if any echo ghostly thin
Survive of me for men to hear at eve
When the boughs tremble as the sunbeams leave,
That echo thy dear name shall tremble in.

For singing ever of thee and rarest things
That make the earth a perfume and a song.
And of vague solace of imaginings,
Thou wilt so closely unto these belong.
That they will tell thy name as with a tongue,
And bring the sighs thy poet's passion brings.

NOTES BY W. M. ROSSETTI

A Vision of Linnaeas
This relates to Tupper's statue of Linnaeas, executed for the Oxford University Museum (see the Prefatory Note). Linnaeus is here represented as quite a young man, clad in skins suited for a traveller in semi-arctic regions: he is abstractedly contemplating a flower which he has plucked as a specimen.

A Quiet Evening,
This, it will be perceived, is a piece of friendly "chaff," relating to an evening which three members of the Pre-Raphaelite Brotherhood — Stephens, my brother, and myself — spent at the family residence of the Tuppers in South Lambeth. The date must have been in 1850. "John" is Tupper himself; "George" and "Aleck" his brothers. The "rhyme of Hell and Heaven," which Gabriel read, must clearly be his ballad "Sister Helen."

A Grotesque
I need scarcely say that this is absolute intentional nonsense. One may surmise that it was written after Tupper had read some pieces of similar aim by Edward Lear or by Lewis Carroll.

Browning's "Sordello"
This again is "chaff." Tupper was always an extreme — indeed a quite passionate — admirer of Browning, and he revelled in "Sordello," though it may readily be believed that he found the poem difficult in parts.

The Debit Side
This sonnet is a burlesque of a sonnet which I wrote in 1849, which was printed on the cover of each number of "The Germ." "The Debit Side" appears to me to relate to a certain affair in which I, as John Tupper's nominee, took an active part at the time, but I am not at all sure.

To my Friend Holman Hunt,
Tupper inscribed this sonnet on the copy of "The Germ" belonging to Mr. Hunt. "The Germ" was published in 1850, and I give that date to the sonnet; but possibly its true date is later on.

To Frederic Stephens.

The date of this sonnet may be towards 1855, when the leading members of the P.R.B. — I need only specify Millais and Hunt — had triumphed over all opposition; whereas Stephens, who had been an art student along with them, and otherwise a zealous co-operator, had practically relinquished the actual exercise of the painting profession.